Does It All Make Sense?

Does It All Make Sense?

Ten Best Guesses about the Meaning of God and of Life

by

Father Joe Breighner

Tully, Inc.
Annapolis, Maryland

Publisher's Cataloging-in-Publication
(Provided by Quality Books, Inc.)

Breighner, Joseph.

    Does it all make sense? : ten best guesses about the
meaning of God and of life / by Joe Breighner. -- 3rd ed.
    p. cm.
    "Originally published: Maryland: F.A.T.A., Inc.,
1991, 1995"--T.p. verso.
    Includes index.
    Preassigned LCCN: 98-60075
    ISBN: 0-9662393-0-X

    1. Christian life--Catholic authors. 2. Christian life--
Anecdotes. 3. Pastoral theology--Catholic Church--Anecdotes.
I. Title.

BX2350.2.B685 1998   248.4'82
                            QBI98-124

Published in 1998 by
Tully, Inc.
1265 Pine Hill Drive
Annapolis, Maryland 21401

Design: Studio Two
Printed in the USA

TABLE OF CONTENTS

Author's Note: *Does It All Make Sense?* has been printed before in two different formats. The first was an 11″ by 14″ booklet with a gold question mark on a white cover. Then it was reprinted in a smaller format, to make it easier to carry and to fit on bookshelves. This third version, with a new cover and new typesetting, is an effort to make the book more readable and accessible to more people. Styles change, but the ideas in this book remain timeless. May this book help you as it has helped so many thousands of other people.

FOREWORD

We have known Father Joe since he was born. We have been with him as he struggled through a childhood without father or security or any privilege. We were there as he agonized through his seminary years, daily doubting his own ability and questioning his value. And we have journeyed with him through the twenty-six years of his ordained ministry, and been there as his philosophy of God and life evolved.

Father Joe writes out of his own experience and his own pain. More than anyone else we know, he can empathize with those who don't love themselves because he was there himself for so many years. His new-found peace was hard-won and much-deserved.

Father Joe's message of love of God and self and others is not new. It was first delivered some 2,000 years ago by a carpenter from Nazareth. Our hope is that the message, so powerful in its simplicity yet so often dismissed, will become more real to the reader through Father Joe's gentle and loving and humorous treatment of it.

So, when you find yourself faced with yet another of life's many challenges, think of this little book. It has been designed to be read in whole or in part, and at least one of the chapters might offer you just the insight or comfort you need at any given moment.

This book, then, is for everyone who has ever felt pain or loss or despair. It is for everyone who is trying to make sense out of a seemingly senseless existence. And it is for everyone who wants to be all that they were meant to be.

It has been our privilege to be some small part of the preparation of this book. It was a labor of love for us, a very small gift for the brother who reminds us so much of yet another Brother.

Helen and Mike Eder
Editors of the First Edition

INTRODUCTION

For the past twenty-three years, I have written and produced a weekly, nationally-syndicated radio show, *The Country Road* — a half-hour mix of country music and my reflections on life. At the same time I have also done a weekly column in a Baltimore newspaper, *The Catholic Review*. In response to the column and the radio show, I receive remarks from all across the country such as:

"You make God so believable."
"You make so much sense of life."

Along with the kind comments are the inevitable questions:

"How does a good God allow bad things to happen?"
"If God is love, why do we have so many laws?"

Occasionally, someone will even ask, "Have you ever written a book about any of these topics?"

This book is an effort to respond in a very simple format to these questions and comments. Twenty-three years of radio scripts and newspaper columns now weigh several pounds and fill a couple of boxes. Rather than try to reproduce all of that material, I would rather try to summarize my philosophy of life that undergirds all that I have spoken and written. Quite simply, I hope to help you make sense of your life by sharing some thoughts about life, love, God, and people which help me to make sense of my own life.

There's a true story about a Lutheran pastor who went to a nursing home to visit an elderly gentleman. This particular man had just had all of his teeth removed, so the pastor figured that he would have to do most of the talking. The pastor arrived around lunch time; as he was speaking to the man, he noticed a dish of peanuts on the man's bedside table. He took a couple of peanuts and, as he talked, continued to pop down one peanut after another, until he suddenly realized that he had eaten the whole dish! Profoundly apologetic, the pastor said to the patient,

"I'm terribly sorry, but I just ate all of your peanuts."

"That's okay," the old man replied with a toothless grin, "before you got here I sucked all the chocolate off of them."

In life sometimes we fall short. The best efforts of churches and individuals to make God believable sometimes have the exact opposite result. In this book I am not attempting to convince anyone to believe as I do. I'm simply offering my best efforts at understanding God and life in a way that makes sense to me. Having spent twelve years in a seminary preparing for ministry, and having spent another twenty-six years as an ordained priest, I realize that many of the things I was taught have not been helpful to others. I have had to rethink and re-understand many of the doctrines and dogmas of faith. My "best guesses" about life are written as a pastor trying to help others, not as an apologist trying to convert them.

Several years ago I had the privilege of officiating at a wedding in which the groom was 72 and the bride was 76! Prior to the wedding, the groom extended me an invitation: "We're having the reception down at the Horn and Horn Cafeteria," he said. "You know," he added wisely, "you can't please everyone. This way people can take whatever they want." I hope many will approach this book as a sort of spiritual smorgasbord — take what you want. Some ideas may be more helpful than others. Some ideas will feed you better than others. The aim of this book is not to provoke quarrels among believers and non-believers, between theologians and church-going people. Enough time has been wasted on that. The aim of this book is to help you feel better about God, about yourself, and about other people. If I succeed even slightly in doing that, then my time has been well spent.

CHAPTER ONE
The God I Believe In

The God I believe in is a God far distant from the image of God I grew up with, or the image of God presented in my early seminary training.

This God was mean, rigid, and demanding. This image of God provoked fear, guilt, and scrupulosity — an unholy trinity! Sadly, it was the indwelling of this image of God that stole so much joy and peace from my youth. To give this image of God credit, it did get my attention and let me know that God was a reality to be taken seriously. Unfortunately, this image of God never allowed room for growth. Life was a matter of constantly straining to do the right thing, holding your breath for fear of failure, and, of course, rushing right to confession if you did fail. Confession would temporarily relieve the guilt, but it was only temporary, since shame and guilt do more to perpetuate behavior patterns than to change them.

A God of guilt, at some point, ceases to be believable. Who wants to spend eternity with such a God, much less spend any time

A God of guilt, at some point, ceases to be believable.

here on earth with Him? I'm reminded of the story of the priest saying in his sermon, "Now I want all of you who would like to go to heaven this morning to stand up." Everybody stood except one young man. Thinking the young man had not heard him, the priest repeated himself. The young man remained seated while the rest of the congregation stood. After Mass the priest button-holed the young man and said, "When I asked everyone who wants to go to heaven this morning to stand, you remained seated. Don't you want to go to heaven?" "Oh, sure, I want to go to heaven," the young man replied, "but I thought all of you were going this morning."

When we are afraid to meet God, then there is something wrong with our notion of God. The God I believe in today is a God almost too good to be described. I agree with the person who said that the only true reason to be an agnostic is that the message of Christianity seems too good to be true. The God I believe in is a God of unconditional love, the Creator-Mother-Father who brought us into being in an explosion of creative love. God is the good shepherd who is with us in the dark times of life, leading us through life's valleys all the way to the mountain peaks of joy and light. God is the father looking for the prodigal son, longing for us more than we long for Him. God is the forgiving God who defends the woman caught in adultery from the crowd who wants to stone her. God is a God of unconditional love who tells us to love each other without condition so that we may find the way to life and peace.

In a moment of candor, a man who was coming to me for spiritual direction once asked, "When did God's love become unconditional?" I replied that I thought it was always unconditional, but we humans, in our interpretation of it, made it very conditional. Too often, I think, we shrink God down to our human level, since we cannot see Him as He really is.

While it is true that many choose to interpret the Bible very narrowly, I see in the Bible a God constantly trying to expand our vision of Him. In the Hebrew scriptures, what we often call the Old Testament, we see interesting expansions. Originally, God was thought of as just the God of one location. When a nation or tribe conquered a territory, it not only took the place, but also took the gods of that place. Yet, when the Jews were carried off into exile, it was the prophets who proposed an expanded notion of God to help the Jews in exile realize that their God went with them. God was no longer confined to the human understanding of one place; rather, God would go where His people went. And while the people of Israel believed that they were especially chosen by God, prophets such as Isaiah helped them to expand their notion of God further, and to realize that they were to be a "light to the nations."

In the Christian scriptures, what we commonly call the New Testament, we see Jesus constantly expanding the vision of God. When people ask Him to stay in one village, He says that He must go on to the next. When the apostles complain that people not of their group are casting out devils, Jesus replies that "he who is not against you is for you." In the early days of the church, as the first Christians try to confine Christianity to the Jews, the Spirit of God expands that notion to include the Gentiles as well. Finally, when different branches of Christianity try to confine salvation to a select group or special following, the Book of Revelations holds the vision of heaven in which multitudes that no one could number, of every tribe and nation, would be gathered at God's throne. We humans try to exclude, to say some are in and some out, and try to project those limits onto God. But God always expands those limits. There is room enough in God's heart for all of us.

One of my greatest sadnesses as a priest is to see the confusion caused to honest, searching people by churches and denominations who tear down other churches and denominations. If millions of people still do not believe in God, sadly enough it is often because we who say we believe in a God of love do not act as if we do.

I like to think of God as an inexhaustible diamond with infinite facets. Each of us is able to perceive a part of the beauty of God. Often we mistake our part for the whole reality. Short of criminal behavior, if we judge and condemn the beliefs of others it is often because we have confused our part with the whole. Arrogance may seem to help some in the world of competition, but humility is the key to understanding God. We need to be humble enough to say, "Yes, God has revealed His fullness to us, but that does not mean we have fully comprehended it, nor does it mean that God has not revealed Himself to others in different ways."

Father Anthony de Mello S.J., an Indian priest and psychologist, once challenged a retreat group with the statement that "doubt is infinitely preferable to worship!" When others got upset at that statement, de Mello commented, "Suppose you were on an airplane that a religious terrorist or fanatic was about to blow up in the name of God. Would you not want that person to have some doubt about his or her notion of God?" Sadly, doubt is often associated with weakness, and authoritative faith is often confused with strength. In reality, just the reverse is true. The person who is secure enough to doubt some of his or her beliefs is strong enough to see the beauty, truth, and goodness in the beliefs of others. The person who is rigid and authoritative is often so insecure that he or she cannot tolerate a different way of thinking. Jesus said to enter by the narrow gate; He did not say to live with narrow minds.

I am not suggesting here that doctrines or creeds are unimportant, or that all the peoples of the world should get together and agree to believe nothing. What I am suggesting is that we take our own beliefs seriously, but have respect for the beliefs of others at the same time. Christians need to remember that the people who did not recognize Jesus were those who were absolutely sure they knew who God was — the religious leaders of His day! Sadly, what religious leaders of every day have a tendency to do is to confuse questions about religion with attacks on their authority. Much of the harm done to religion and to the world in the form of persecutions and religious wars has not been done by doubters, but by those too rigid to see the presence of God in people who believe differently.

The God I believe in, then, is quite simply a God far beyond our human capacity to fully comprehend or appreciate. I believe God is far more loving, more caring, more forgiving, than

> **I believe God is far more loving, more caring, than we have ever imagined.**

we have ever imagined. God is not someone we need to fear. Perfect love casts out fear, and God has come to perfect our love.

Believing in a wonderful God makes us wonderful. Cruelty has been done in the name of a cruel God. Kindness is done in the name of a kind God. G. K. Chesterton has said that "Christianity hasn't failed. It just has never been tried." His words could be applied to most religions, since religious ideals are amazingly similar. Love your neighbor as yourself is a Jewish as well as a Christian concept, and it is repeated or echoed in most of the other world religions as well. The fact that so much lack of love exists is a testimony to our human tendency to retreat from God's call to expand ourselves to love, and retreat instead into our fears and pettiness. We humans can be more than we ever dreamed we could be if we would just allow ourselves to believe in a God who is more than we ever dreamed God could be.

Dr. Martin Luther King Jr. once said that "the thing wrong with an eye for an eye is that everybody ends up blind." Strict justice is often just a nicer name for revenge. Revenge gets us nowhere in our personal or public lives. Again, I believe it was King who said that "revenge makes us even but forgiveness makes us better." Yes, in the real world we need police and military and prisons to protect civilized people from the potential ravages of the sociopath and the psychopath and the criminal element. But the more we can expand our notion of God, the more we can expand our notion of our potential as humans. Rather than being ruled by the fears of our worst behavior, we can multiply our good behavior. If God is as good as God says He is, and I believe He is, then I believe that with God's spirit in us we can love and live and care and give and forgive in ways we never dreamed of. We will never know how good we are until we can believe how good God is!

CHAPTER TWO
Heaven and Hell

My second guess about life is that heaven and hell are the same place.

My favorite story about heaven and hell is about the priest giving a hell, fire, and damnation sermon one Sunday, and at the end of his sermon he said, "Now I would like all of you who want to go to heaven to stand up." The whole church stood. The priest looked around, feeling satisfied with the impression he was making, and asked the congregation to be seated. In a very somber tone, the priest then asked, "Now, I would like all of you who want to go to hell to stand up." No one moved. The priest stood there looking around at his congregation, again feeling good about the impression he was making, when suddenly a man in the last pew stood up! Flustered, the priest scratched his head, leaned into the microphone, and asked, "Sir, do you really want to go to hell?" "No, Father, I don't," the man replied. "I just felt embarrassed for you since you were the only person standing."

I believe hell is what we sentence ourselves to. Quite simply, heaven is living with God; hell is trying to live without Him. Every

> **I believe hell is what we sentence ourselves to.**

day we are aware of people in dehumanizing and degrading situations who still manage to live with a degree of serenity and peace because they sense the presence of God with them. Conversely, we know of other people who live in apparent splendor and luxury whose lives are miserable. They manage to turn a rose garden into a cemetery, because without an awareness of God's presence, life is meaningless and empty.

For years I struggled as a priest and counselor with the notion of hell. People have stayed in abusive relationships and perpetuated self-destructive behavior because, in their religious belief system, failure to do so could doom them to hell. I found the notion of hell, the notion that an all-loving God could condemn us to a place of pain forever, as being contradictory to the notion of an all-loving God. That God would bribe us with heaven and scare us with hell seemed somehow unworthy of God.

Yet, at the same time, I was aware of evil in its rawest forms. The Hitlers and Stalins who doomed millions to death and who brought destruction to the world: would they not qualify as candidates for such a place as hell? I was torn between the reality of hell, which might be the only brake on certain people's destructive behavior, and the notion of hell, which was torturing good people with scrupulosity and obsessive fears about sin and final damnation. How could I reconcile the notion of a good God, who would not want to scare good people with the threat of hell, with the notion of a God who, in strict justice, would have to treat a Hitler differently than a Mother Theresa?

Through years of prayer and reading and meditating, I came to realize that we sentence ourselves to hell. A key to my thinking came when I heard a Jewish rabbi say something to the effect that "the reward for the good deed is the good deed." As children, we think when we do something good that mommy or daddy or teacher or someone in authority should pat us on the head and praise us. Since many people never grow beyond a childish concept of God (not to be confused with a childlike concept of God), it would be easy for organized religion to package God as a good daddy who rewards good behavior or an angry daddy who punishes bad behavior. This works fine until people grow up in their faith and as adults start to think about God. Childish notions do not satisfy adult thinking.

As adults we can appreciate the wisdom of what the rabbi said. The reward of the good deed is that we did the right thing. We become better people and the world becomes a better place if we have behaved in loving and caring ways. To do the right thing simply because it is the right thing

To do the right thing simply because it is the right thing is its own reward.

is its own reward, even if no one else notices or likes what we did. Someone once commented that "no good deed goes unpunished." As children we think that if we are good, the world will be good to us. As adults we realize that doing good brings no guarantee of reward. If there was ever a better person than Jesus of Nazareth, I don't know who it was, yet He was treated abusively by religious and civil authorities. He was treated poorly even by His friends. Still, Jesus lived with a constant awareness of His Father's presence which enabled Him to experience heaven in the midst of hellish treatment.

On the other hand, we know all too well the hell our destructive behavior can bring. We have only to think about the pain and destruction brought about by alcohol and drug addiction and other addictive behaviors. The cure for so much of our self-destructive behavior begins with acknowledging our powerlessness and turning our lives over to a Higher Power. By inviting the presence of God into our personal hells, we can turn hell into heaven.

Concretely, when I speak of heaven and hell being the same place, what image do I have of eternity? I love the image offered by the parable of the man who asked God to let him see heaven and hell. God agreed. In the first scene the man saw hell. It consisted of people seated at tables with large platters of delicious foods piled on them. Each person, however, had long forks and spoons tied to the ends of their hands, utensils so long that they could not bring the food up to their mouths. So everyone at the table was hungry and complaining and angry. Then God showed the man a vision of heaven. Much to the man's surprise, he saw the same setting! There were people seated at tables piled high with food, with long spoons and forks attached to the ends of their hands. However, everyone was happy and cheerful and well-fed. The difference was that while the situation was the same, instead of being frustrated and angry, each person was putting food on his or her spoon or fork and then reaching over to feed the person across the table. People who had been unselfish continued to be unselfish and people who had been selfish continued to be selfish. The place was the same, but the choice of behavior made it either heaven or hell.

How do I view our particular judgment at the end of life? I think when each person comes into the presence of God, that person experiences His presence differently. Let's look at two possibilities — Mother Theresa of Calcutta and Adolf Hitler.

At the end of her life, when Mother Theresa came into the presence of God, I believe that she experienced that presence as warmth and love. She who devoted herself untiringly to unselfishness and caring about others experienced the love coming back to her from the presence of God. Hitler, on the other hand, may have come into that same presence, but rather than experience it as warmth and light, may have experienced it as fire and pain. What one person experiences as burning love, another experiences as burning fire. Because of a lifetime of selfishness and cruelty and destructiveness, Hitler's reaction to love is fear;

his reaction to light is to hide; his reaction to total unselfish love is shame and guilt. In other words, by his life's choices Hitler conditioned himself to a very different experience of God than did Mother Theresa. In each case, the reality is the same, but the experience of it was conditioned by personal choices throughout life. Heaven begins with opening ourselves to God's loving presence during life, thus preparing ourselves to embrace that presence at the end of life. Hell in this life is trying to live without God. Hell in the next life is the same choice!

Again, our understanding of heaven and hell relates to our understanding of God. Most often, the distortions we project onto God are caused by our human limitations in understanding a God of unconditional love. Our understanding of hell often involves projecting our human limitations on that concept as well. Too often our need for revenge, or condemning others, or judging others, is what we project onto God. We create God in our image, rather than allow God to recreate us in His image. When we allow ourselves a new understanding of God, we discover a new understanding of our beliefs and doctrines and especially a new understanding of the Bible.

> **Our understanding of hell often involves our need for revenge, or condemning others, or judging others.**

18

On the light side, when I think of judging and human limitations, I think of the story of the couple who appeared before St. Peter at the gates of heaven. St. Peter asked the man what he died of, and the man replied, "Seen us." St. Peter corrected him, "You mean sinus!" "No," the man replied. "I mean seen us. I was out with my best friend's wife and he seen us." (Sometimes, in my choice of stories, you can tell that I have been doing a radio show with country music for over twenty years!)

When you and I can get past our human notions of revenge and getting even, we can begin to realize that God has no such needs. I can't conceive of a God who would be glorified by human beings suffering in eternal pain. Even I, a weak and fallible person, cannot conceive of anyone whom I would want to punish forever. Even those who support capital punishment are not likely to want a person to suffer pain forever. If we humans with all of our limitations have a hard time imagining anyone we would want to punish forever, how can we imagine a God who would want that? Again, a God who would bribe us with thoughts of heaven and scare us with thoughts of hell does not seem like a God worthy of worship. That sounds more like the kind of God humans would create to control other people.

A God of love, however, is not a God who wants to get even, but a God who wants to make better. I do not consider the tragedies of life (a topic I will discuss in a later chapter) to be punishments from God but, rather, opportunities for us to become better people by coping with tragedies and coming closer to God. That we might experience burning love in eternity as burning fire as a result of our choices during life seems to open the possibility that pain may not be an eternal state. Perhaps it may take time, even a very long time, before the love of God can burn away our sins, fears, guilt, and shame and we come to realize that we are not in the bowels of hell but in the arms of love. If God wants to make life better, then a love that transforms us in eternity seems more worthy of Him than a God who punishes for all eternity. I think God is that good.

CHAPTER THREE
We Are Better Than We Think We Are

My third best guess about life is that people are better than we sometimes think they are. We are better than we often think we are. Part of the tragedy of life today is that instant communication brings to our living rooms scenes of murder and terrorism and mayhem from around the country and around the world. There is simply no way that we can constantly read and hear and watch stories of muggings and rapes and thefts without it beginning to affect our personal worlds. We start to view other people with suspicion. We wonder whom we can and cannot trust. We wonder where we can and cannot go.

Yet, if we are honest, we have to admit that good outweighs evil many millions of times every day! The news accounts report stories of tragedy and destruction because, fortunately, those stories are still the exception. We do not see headlines such as "Boy Hugs Dog"; "Man And Woman Promise Love For Life"; "Teacher Helps Student." These are not news stories because they are not the exception, they are the rule. If we do start seeing headlines like these then we had better start worrying, because it would mean that good would be the exception to the rule!

Just as beauty is in the eye of the beholder, so often good or bad is in the eye of the beholder. One of my favorite stories about mis-

People are better than we sometimes think they are.

judging others is a true story that the great Bishop Fulton Sheen once told about himself. This internationally-famous radio and TV personality and lecturer of the 1950s and '60s was riding on a subway one day in New York. At one particular stop a disreputable-looking gentleman reeking of booze and b.o. boarded the subway and plopped down in a seat next to Bishop Sheen. This man's eyes were glassy, and he just stared at the newspaper he was holding. Finally, he turned to Bishop Sheen and asked, "How does a man get diabetes?" Figuring this was his chance to really nail him, Bishop Sheen responded sarcastically, "A man gets diabetes from drinking too much, and neglecting his responsibilities." As soon as the words were out, the good Bishop experienced remorse. "I should not have put this man down like that," Bishop Sheen thought to himself. So, in an effort to restart the conversation, Bishop Sheen turned to the man and asked, "Tell me. Why did you ask me that question?" The man looked up from his newspaper and replied, "I was just reading that the Pope has diabetes."

In life it can be very dangerous to judge other people. As the old saying goes, "Whenever we point a finger at someone else, there are three fingers pointing back at us." Too often when we think the worst of others, we are simply masking some negative feelings about ourselves. As Shakespeare once said so profoundly, "The problem is not in our stars but in ourselves."

One of the most helpful insights into human behavior comes from a theory that a Johns Hopkins University psychiatrist, Dr. Milton Layden, articulated in a book entitled *Escaping the Hostility Trap*. His theory was refined by a group called Human Equations who specializes in employee training seminars. Briefly, the theory is boiled down to a single equation:

$$I \rightarrow A = H.$$

The I stands for feelings of inferiority or feelings of inadequacy. Feelings of inferiority result in A, which stands for anxiety. The result is H, hostility. Thus feelings of inferiority produce anxiety, and the result is hostility. Hostility is how we protect ourselves, how we compensate or cover up our feelings of inadequacy. (Let me hasten to add that this theory is not meant to be the only explanation for anger. There is also something known as primary anger, when anger is an appropriate expression. For example, much of the social change that has occurred throughout history comes from anger at injustices. This theory simply attempts to point out that often in human relationships our anger serves to cover our feelings of inadequacy and is not a search for justice.)

While it would take a book in itself to fully explain the theory, let's go back to the story of the bishop and the drunk. What Bishop Sheen was not aware of was how much anxiety the drunk sitting next to him was pro-

If we are angry, it impairs our ability to hear what someone else is saying to us.

voking. Sheen was unaware of his own prejudices about drinking, and did not hear the man's real question; instead, he dumped his anger on the man. The drunk responded in kind. Sheen's response had furthered the man's feelings of inadequacy and inferiority, he felt more anxious, and his response was equally hostile. The story not only illustrates the basic validity of the theory that feelings of inferiority and anxiety result in hostility, but also confirms a second theory: When hostility is high, receptivity is low. In other words, if we are angry, it impairs our ability to hear what someone else is saying to us. Our anger blocks us from receiving the message.

In that little equation, then, lies an explanation for so much of the pain in relationships and families, and even an explanation of warfare between nations. Any time someone attacks us, we feel a lowered sense of self-worth, an increased level of anxiety, and we compensate by retaliating from hostility. Feuds between the Hatfields and McCoys, battles between Catholics and Protestants in Ireland, and continued bloodshed between Jews and Arabs in the Middle East are tragic confirmations that we can stay stuck in hostile behavior without ever dealing with the source.

What is the source? The only source for healing lies in overcoming our feelings of inferiority or inadequacy. We need to build up our sense of self-worth and self-esteem. As individuals, that may mean doing simple exercises such as taking a few moments at the beginning of each day to recall times when we felt good about ourselves, felt successful, felt helpful to others. As we restore our self-esteem, we lower our anxiety and consequently our hostility. Because our hostility is lowered, we are better able to hear what others are saying to us, and we do not feel a need to respond in anger. As nations and factions and groups, we may need to rebuild our self-esteem by finding our worth not in the territory we hold, but in the values we hold. When we call forth the best in ourselves, we find it easier to see the good in others.

One reality remains true. We generally find it hard to love others if we do not love ourselves. Perhaps we all have to go back to the wisdom of the little boy in religion class who said, "God made me, and God don't make junk." Only as we value ourselves can we value someone else. One of the tragedies of this "me" generation is that self-love is often confused with selfishness. Nothing could be farther from the truth. Selfishness says, "I look out for me and tough for you." Self-love says, "I learn to value me so that I can more fully value you."

Eric Hoffer, the practical philosopher, once wrote, "It is not love of self, but hatred of self, which is at the root of the troubles that afflict the world." While the roots of our lack of self-love, the roots of our sense of inadequacy and inferiority, may go back to childhood and early life experiences and require professional counseling or therapy, there are thoughts and attitudes that can help us right now. As a help to believing that thinking the best of others comes from thinking the best of ourselves, I would like to share what I call my Ten Commandments of Self-Love.

I   You shall love yourself because your self is a part of God's self. You have been made in the image and likeness of God. Love yourself because you are a reflection of God.

II   You shall love yourself even if someone else does not love you. We humans can make weak and fallible judgments. God, however, is infallible and He loves you with an eternal love.

III   You shall love yourself even if you fail or sin. Guilt is meant to be a reminder of failure, but it is not a state we are meant to live in. Learning from the past and changing our attitudes and behaviors make us more like God than wallowing in guilt.

IV   You shall love yourself more than your fears. Fear will steal life from you. God wants you to have the fullness of life. Faith is stronger than fear.

V   You shall love yourself in times of despair. Feelings of despair will pass if we cling to hope in God who will last forever.

VI   You shall love yourself enough to give yourself away. Just as we cannot separate ourselves from God, we cannot separate ourselves from others. As you give to others, so you give to God and so you act like God.

VII   You shall love yourself because God wants to take on your personal self. Just as we Christians believe that God took on flesh and blood and was born in Bethlehem, so God wants to take on your flesh and blood and be born in you. Respect the temple of God that you are.

VIII   You shall love yourself because God is love. When you love yourself, you give glory to God.

IX   You shall love yourself because God has loved you. If you were the only person in the world, God would have been born, suffered, and died just for you. If God loves you so, why would you ever dare not to love you?

X   You shall love yourself because God wouldn't want a world without you. God could have chosen to create such a world, but a world without you just wasn't the kind of world God wanted. God wants you here. Why would you ever doubt your purpose?

It's so easy to write and read words about self-love, but often so hard to love ourselves. Yet therein lies the secret of personal peace, and therein lies the hope for world peace. Anthony de Mello has written, "It is easier to wear slippers than to try to carpet the world." When we can cushion our own self-criticism, we find it easier to cushion our criticism of others. If we can believe that we are good and special, that we have God's light and life shining in us, then we sense that we are not diminished by sharing that life and seeing that light in others. A wise person stated, "You do not have to blow out someone else's candle to make your light shine brighter." Too often that is precisely what we do. In our self-hatred we "put out someone else's light." In our self-love we want to share the light. It's true that we will not always live up to such noble ideals, but how much sadder the world would be if we did not try.

CHAPTER FOUR
The Ten Commandments

My fourth best guess about life is that the ten commandments protect us from sinking below our ideals. Someone commented that the story of Moses and the ten commandments was the first record of a headache. That is because the Bible recorded that Moses came down the mountain carrying two tablets!

For many of us commandments seem more like a headache than a blessing. Who wants to be told what to do? Too often, perhaps, the commandments seem to say that God first looked at us humans to see what we liked to do, and then said we could not do it. I recall the apocryphal story of Moses returning to his people after they had complained bitterly about all the commandments and Moses had decided to go back and bargain with God. When Moses returned again to the people, he said, "I've got some good news and some bad news. The good news is that I got God down to only ten commandments. The bad news is that number six is still on the list."

Commandments are a reminder that we humans have a dark side. Yes, God's love is unconditional, but our response to that love is often very conditional. God did not give us the commandments for His sake, but for ours. We need to have something by which we can measure our response to God's love. I still recall the words of an old pastor during the 1960s when so much antiwar protesting and civil disobedience was going on. He said, "All I hear about is the Catonsville Nine and the Harrisburg Seven. What about the Sinai Ten?"

Commandments are a reminder that we humans have a dark side.

For those who may not be able to recall the Sinai Ten, they are found in the first 17 verses of Chapter 20 in the Book of Exodus. Here is a condensed list:

1   I, the Lord, am your God, who brought you out of the land of Egypt, that place of slavery. You shall not have other gods besides me.

2   You shall not take the name of the Lord, your God, in vain.

3   Remember to keep holy the sabbath day.

4   Honor your father and your mother.

5   You shall not kill.

6   You shall not commit adultery.

7   You shall not steal.

8   You shall not bear false witness against your neighbor.

9   You shall not covet your neighbor's wife.

10 You shall not covet your neighbor's goods.

As the Bible records the commandments, there are both blessings and threats included. While I believe in a God of unconditional love, there are people who live life at a childish level. As emotional children they respond only to rewards or punishments. They are not inspired by a God of love to respond lovingly and many confuse love with weakness. So the ten commandments are phrased in such a way that both the least aware and the most aware can profit from them.

In listing the commandments I am certainly not attempting to bring back much of the real or imagined guilt that many associate with them. As someone once said, "Puritanism didn't keep the Puritans from sinning. It just kept them from enjoying it." In a very real sense, the commandments won't keep people from breaking them. However, in having minimum standards of human conduct, at least we will be able to know when we have fallen below the minimum.

I believe the commandments are of enduring value because they continue to remind us of important values to preserve and behaviors to avoid. No less a figure than Ted Koppel has stated, in a commencement address, that all the ills of

> **The commandments continue to remind us of important values to preserve and behaviors to avoid.**

society could be traced back to some violation of the ten commandments. We may change the names, but the realities remain the same. Insider trading, corporate greed, and petty theft still come under "Thou shalt not steal." Political careers ruined because of affairs and families destroyed because of sexual acting out still fall under "Thou shalt not commit adultery." Wars, terrorism, and murders still come under "Thou shalt not kill." Pollution of the air, land, and sea are reminders that we have not kept God's name or His creation holy but have indeed taken them in vain. (Which reminds me of a time not long ago when I visited a race track with a friend. As he and I watched the horses and the people, one man nearby continued a string of G.D.'s and Jesus Christ's and so on. I turned to my friend and commented wryly, "I don't think God did all He did so that one day we could all stand around a race track and take His name in vain!")

Without wanting to belabor race tracks, which I have visited about six times in my life, I also recall the story of the man watching a priest down in the stable area praying over horses. Before each race the priest prayed over a particular horse and then that horse went out and won the race. After watching three races, the man put every penny he had on the horse he saw the priest praying over before the fourth race. When the race began, the horse took two steps out of the starting gate and dropped dead! Infuriated, the man raced over to the priest and demanded to know what had gone wrong. The priest responded calmly, "Nothing went wrong. You apparently do not know the difference between a blessing and the last rites!"

Many people really do find the "religion thing" very confusing. They are put off by rituals and vestments and worship services and commandments. Let me try to break religion down to its simplest components. None of the parts, including commandments, make sense without a picture of the whole.

I use a very simple drawing when I try to give an overview of my concept of religion. First, I draw a circle and in the circle I place a J or G. If I'm talking to a Christian audience, I use the J for Jesus. Jesus is at the center of our life, and life will make sense depending on the depth of our relationship with Him. If I'm talking to a non-Christian audience, I put a G in the circle for God. God is at the center of our life, and life will make sense to us depending on our relationship with Him (or Her). Around the circle I then write three things: self-esteem, self-discipline, and self-giving. If God or Jesus is at the center of our lives, then those three realities will reflect that relationship. First, we will have self-esteem, which I went into at some length in the last chapter. Let me hasten to add, however, that low self-esteem does not necessarily reflect a lack of faith; it may simply reflect our many negative life experiences which still influence how we feel about ourselves. Self-esteem, however, is what we deserve to have from our relationship with God, and our self-esteem will be aided by that relationship.

Self-esteem, however, is not enough. As I mentioned earlier, we all have a "dark side." We do not always live up to our ideals, nor are we always touched or motivat-

Self-esteem without self-discipline can easily deteriorate into selfishness.

ed by love. In our competitive society, high self-esteem is easily turned in selfishness: "I feel good about me, so I'm going to get all I can for me!" While this is not true self-esteem, it shows how the notion of self-esteem can be prostituted by our other cravings, such as lust and greed. Self-esteem without self-discipline can easily deteriorate into selfishness. That's why we always need to balance the Commandments of Love of God and Neighbor with the Ten Commandments so that our failures to love will be obvious.

But self-discipline is not enough, either. We all know people who keep all the laws, but would be the last people we would ever go to for understanding or compassion. There are those who confuse rigidity with divinity. Ironically, the people who gave Jesus the hardest time, the religious leaders of His day, were not undisciplined people. They kept all the laws; they had simply forgotten that the purpose of the law was not to make them self-righteous, but righteous. They had forgotten the relationship with God that was the purpose behind their self-discipline. So, just as self-esteem needs self-discipline to keep from devolving into selfishness, so self-discipline needs self-giving to keep from deteriorating into rigidity and self-righteousness.

Most of us are not aware of how selfishly we may be living. It's hard to give of ourselves. There is a wonderful passage in the book *In Africa with Schweitzer* by Dr. Edgar Berman. Near the end of his stay in Africa with the Nobel Peace Prize winner and religious humanitarian Albert Schweitzer, Dr. Berman records this conversation:

(Schweitzer)   "If the Church could teach its faithful how to live better, it wouldn't have to teach them how to die. How can most of us die peacefully if in our hearts we are cognizant of how selfishly we have lived?"

(Berman)   "But, Dr. Schweitzer, most of us don't want to realize how selfishly we live; we rationalize it on the basis of family, success, or just plain survival."

(Schweitzer)   "And that's what is so wrong. The rationalization
                — going along with the herd, not being an indi-
                vidual."

Self-giving moves us beyond selfishness and rigidity. The Gospels
sum this up best when Jesus states, "Greater love no one has than
to lay down his life for his friends." It is ironic that when we give
of ourselves, we get both peace and satisfaction. Many Biblical
scholars see the contrast between the Dead Sea and the Sea of
Galilee as a parable. The Sea of Galilee is teeming with life
because water flows into it and out of it. The sea receives and
gives. The Dead Sea is dead because while water flows in, nothing flows out. It dies and stagnates. There is no life for a body that
does not give of itself.

In our lives, then, we need to believe how good God is so that we
can discover how good we are. Our self-esteem grows from knowing how much God esteems us. And since we are capable of dis-
figuring the image of God in ourselves and in others, we need the
commandments to serve as checks on our destructive impulses.
However, self-esteem and self-discipline can keep us preoccupied
just with ourselves, so we need self-giving to move us beyond ourselves into caring about others.

We learn from the Scriptures that God saves His people. We are
in this together. Health and happiness come when we move from
the "me generation" into the "we generation."

CHAPTER FIVE

No Sin Is Unforgivable

My fifth best guess about life is that no sin is unforgivable. So much life is stolen from people by guilt. Nothing brings more pain to my life as a minister of the Gospel and pastoral counselor than continually to meet people who feel unforgiven. Part of the reason I chose to follow the chapter on commandments with this chapter is that some people cannot hear the words law or sin or commandment without being thrown into depression and guilt. One man was so scrupulous, so obsessed with his sense of sin and guilt, that the only thing that brought him peace was to resign himself to hell! He concluded that, since he spent so much time worrying about sin and hell, if he resigned himself to damnation he could at least live without continuing daily to beat himself up with his hyperactive conscience.

When damning ourselves to hell brings more peace than God then there is something dramatically wrong with our concept of God. To believe that no sin is unforgivable is simply to accept the fact that God is bigger than any sin, and His mercy is greater than our failures. Ironically, we humans often have a hard time accepting God's forgiveness because we have never forgiven ourselves. So I want to reflect on forgiveness under three headings:

1. Self-forgiveness;
2. God's forgiveness;
3. Forgiveness of others.

When I think of self-forgiveness, I recall the story of the little boy asking his teacher if she would punish him for something he had not done. She replied, "Of course I would not punish you for something you did not do." The boy responded triumphantly, "That's good, because I didn't do my homework." When we think of sin and forgiveness, we usually begin by thinking of an authority figure outside ourselves handing out a punishment or commuting a sentence. Yet the worst judge is often the judge within. Later in this book I will devote a whole chapter to the enemy within. Suffice it to say here that if we do not forgive ourselves, we may never really allow ourselves to accept God's forgiveness. If we do not accept God the way God is, we may never accept ourselves the way we are. If we are self-critical, we may even be critical of God.

> **If we do not accept God the way God is, we may never accept ourselves the way we are.**

I recall a story that was purported to be true. Two clergymen were arguing about drinking. One clergyman in exasperation finally blurted out, "My gosh, man, even Jesus drank wine." Unimpressed, the other clergyman replied, "Yes, but I would have thought more of Him if He hadn't." Sometimes we shrink God to our level of understanding rather than dare to expand ourselves to God's level. As Mother Theresa of Calcutta put it, "Prayer is expanding our hearts to make room for God."

Self-forgiveness opens up the way to receiving God's forgiveness. Many of us, however, refuse to forgive ourselves. We list our sins, real or imagined, and decide that we are awful. We may even be able to say the words, "God forgives me," but we never allow ourselves to forgive us.

What are some things that help self-forgiveness? First, we need to accept the fact that we humans have a right to be wrong! By that I simply mean that for centuries Christianity has articulated the doctrine of original sin. I don't intend to get into a theological discussion of that. It simply means that something went wrong at the very beginning and we have inherited the tendency to do things wrong. Ruth Tiffany Barnhouse, an Episcopal priest and psychiatrist, defined original sin as "that which renders us incapable of always making the right decision." If we can accept the fact that there is a tendency in us to make bad choices it can sometimes be easier for us to forgive those bad choices.

Second, we need to accept the fact that God loves us as we are, and that we do not give glory to God by punishing ourselves. Christians have heard the words of Jesus to Peter that we are to forgive others seventy times seven but we have never accepted the fact that we can forgive ourselves an infinite number of times. We may punish ourselves from a false sense of penance or atonement, but that simply drags us down; it does not glorify God. God would much prefer that I use the energy I am wasting on guilt and self-punishment to help others. Ironically, knowing that I am loved as I am, with all my failings and weaknesses and imperfections, is what makes it possible to change and to be better. Sadly, most of us torture ourselves out of a sense of personal dissatisfaction rather than accept ourselves as an act of faith in God. It is feeling loved that makes us come alive and sets us free, not being self-critical. As a wise person put it, "Make the decision that God is benevolent," and then be benevolent toward yourself.

Self-forgiveness opens up the way to accept God's forgiveness. God's forgiveness does what we cannot do for ourselves. God changes things forever. I'm reminded of a time I was pouring the water over a baby's head in Baptism, and the baby's big sister, who was watching intently, said, "Father Joe, don't forget to wash behind the ears." God washes behind the ears; He does what we cannot do for ourselves.

No matter how often we have sinned, God forgives and will forgive. No matter how "big" our sins seem to us, God forgives. No matter how terrible we may feel about any failings and sins,

No matter how often we have sinned, God forgives and will forgive.

God forgives. There is no limit to God's mercy. The only limit is the limit we put on ourselves in accepting God's mercy.

In my understanding of God, God forgives because sinning is not the most important activity of life. Loving is the most important activity of life, and God wants to set us free from sin to do what really counts — loving and caring about someone else.

I believe that just as Jesus was aware that He was the Son of God, and that understanding affected everything He said and did, so we must discover that we, too, are sons and daughters of God. The challenge of life is not to discover how bad we are, but to discover how good we are. God wants to set us free, not leave us running around in circles of guilt.

I often define sin as an "identity crisis." If I do something hurtful to myself, something unworthy of a son or daughter of God, then I have forgotten my own dignity. If I do something to you not worthy of the treatment of a son or daughter of God, I have forgotten your dignity. Sin is forgetting who we are, and acting in ways that do not reflect our innate dignity. Salvation is being told

41

who we are, and given the grace and love to be different.

Too often I hear the expression that we need to "convict people of sin." While I understand the desire of people to call others to repentance, I think rather we are called to convict people of goodness. Convicting people of sin often keeps people in a pattern of sin and shame because one reality simply reinforces the other. However, if we can convict people of their goodness, of believing how good they are, then they can surrender destructive patterns of behavior from a sense of self-worth, rather than repeating destructive patterns from a lack of self-worth. I recall a lady who always went to Mass celebrated by a priest who invariably gave hell, fire, and damnation sermons. When I asked her one day why she always went to his service, she responded, "Oh, he always makes me feel like dirt." Being convinced of her sinfulness did not change her. It simply kept her in a mind-set of low self-esteem. Trying to convince her that God took dirt and breathed His Spirit into it, that God turned dirt to humans rather than turn humans to dirt, was a difficult process. No doubt her guilt kept her coming to church, but her concept of God never freed her for joy and peace.

In life, then, we need to believe how good we are in order to forgive ourselves. Then we need to believe how good God is in order to accept God's forgiveness. And finally, we need to share forgiveness with someone else. This is sometimes the hardest step, but also a critical one. If we do not want to forgive ourselves, or accept God's forgiveness, perhaps it has something to do with our unwillingness to forgive others. Forgiving others does not always come easy. We will do it imperfectly, just as we do most other things in life. I'm reminded of the religion teacher instructing her class about Jesus telling us to turn the other cheek. After class had finished, she asked little

If we do not want to forgive ourselves, or accept God's forgiveness, perhaps it has something to do with our unwillingness to forgive others.

Johnny, "Now, Johnny, when you go home and the neighbor's boy strikes you on the right cheek, what are you going to do?" Johnny replied, "How big is the neighbor's boy?"

It is seldom easy to forgive others. We have all been victims of real injustices and real pain. Forgiveness of others does not mean forgiving and forgetting. Amnesia is not a virtue. Forgiveness is a decision to let go of our feelings of revenge. Forgiveness is absolving someone else, and freeing ourselves.

Basically we forgive for two reasons. First, we forgive because we believe God has forgiven us. The mercy we receive is the mercy we want to pass on. We forgive because we believe we deserve to act like God. The other person may not appreciate our forgiveness nor even respond to it. But we do it because we believe that is what God would do.

43

Second, we forgive because it is a part of self-love. We all know that if we're angry at someone else, if we're carrying around bitterness and resentment in our hearts, the person we are hurting is not the person we are angry at. The person we are hurting is ourselves. Keeping ourselves stewing and frustrated inside does nothing to the other person, but it sure does a number on us. So if we are having trouble forgiving someone else for the love of God, we might consider forgiving someone else for the love of ourselves. Harboring grudges and resentments is like keeping something dead in our hearts. It takes away the joy of living. It can keep us from feeling like sons and daughters of God.

Let me hasten to add that forgiving others does not mean condoning abuse. Too often good people will say something like, "Well, the Bible says to forgive, so I should forgive this person even though he or she is treating me terribly." When I speak of forgiving others, I am thinking of forgiving someone for some past offense or offenses, not condoning continued bad treatment in the present. If we are allowing someone to treat us poorly, we are actually colluding in our own poor treatment. We deserve better than that. When a person we are in a relationship with ceases their abusive behavior and makes a sincere effort to change, then forgiving their past behavior can make a difference.

Forgiveness can be a complicated issue. Our understanding of forgiveness can be wrapped up in our self-concept, our concept of God, our personality formation, and our relationships. The fact remains that God wants to forgive us even more than we may want to be forgiven. God wants to free us from guilt and shame and fear in order to live life in joy and peace and happiness. If we are experiencing negative feelings rather than positive feelings, the problem may be that we have not really forgiven ourselves or someone else. The problem is not with God. God wants us to live life to the fullest. If we are experiencing something less, then we need to take the risk of changing something in our lives. The one thing that won't change, though, is God's unconditional love and esteem for us.

CHAPTER SIX
Love, Lust, and Friendship

My sixth best guess about life is that we need to associate love with friendship rather than with lust. This may seem a strange supposition in a book aimed at those who may have given up on God, but I believe that it is precisely in losing sight of a healthy concept of God that we lose the ability for healthy relationships between people.

There is no need to document here the destruction done to society and to individuals by confusing lust with love. Suffice it to say that the rise in teen pregnancies, the increase of sexually-transmitted diseases, child abuse, marital breakdowns, and so on, document daily that making love has little to do with real love. Pro-choice and pro-life forces alike agree that abortions are never sought from a spirit of joy.

It is fair to say that ours is a society obsessed with sex. On the light side, when I think of our sexual obsession, I recall a story I read many years ago in *Reader's Digest*. It was about a teacher who found a summer job teaching a course in sex education at a local school. Since he was newly married and did not want to embarrass

It is fair to say that ours is a society obsessed with sex.

his wife by saying he was teaching a course in sex, he told his wife instead that he was teaching a course in sailing. One evening his wife agreed to meet him at the school when he was finished with his class. As she stood outside the classroom, a student was coming out and recognized her. "Oh, your husband is such a wonderful teacher," she blurted out. The wife, again thinking the course was in sailing, responded, "I'm really surprised to hear that, since he doesn't know much about the subject. He only tried it twice. The first time he got sick and the second time he fell off."

We can laugh at the humor associated with sex, but the obsession of our society with sex is hardly a laughing matter. Sadly, we use sex to sell products in our "legitimate" advertising industry, and the multibillion-dollar porno industry uses sex to sell people. People are marketed for our sexual pleasure much as we would market any other product. The result of this media bombardment is that we have become addicted to stimulation. Consequently, we have largely lost our ability as a society to be tender, gentle, caring, responsible, and committed.

The cure, as I see it, is to re-associate love with friendship. I recall a psychiatrist once commenting, "We get married for many reasons but we get divorced for only one reason. We're not friends any more." Volumes are spoken in that statement. Relationships are so shallow and vulnerable today because attraction brings two people together; however, only commitment can keep them together. In our society, we have confused the package with the person. We know how to look good, but not how to be good. We know what styles to wear, but not what virtues to clothe ourselves in. We are obsessed with our weight, with our physical appearance, simply because we have lost any real contact with, or awareness of, our spiritual selves. St. Paul said that "what is seen is transitory. What is unseen lasts forever." Our society has reversed the priorities: "What is seen is important. What is unseen doesn't really matter." Because we have ceased to look for the spiritual dimension in each person, we often miss the divine that is there. Obviously, we humans disagree about God's presence. Some believe we bring God to others. I believe that we bring God out of each other. I love the story and the image of Michelangelo hauling a huge block of marble to carve his famous statue of David. When the townsfolk asked him what he was going to do with that chunk of marble, Michelangelo responded, "There is a man trapped in the marble. I'm going to try to bring him out." Love brings out the God in each of us. Lust without love simply distorts the image of God in each of us. We need to be friends before we are lovers.

Friendship means that we delight in someone else's presence. A friend is someone who knows you the way you are and still likes you! If we marry a friend we marry someone we can build an enduring relationship with. Even if we have married for the wrong reasons, there is often the ability to become friends. Lust is a feeling. Love is a decision. The decision to befriend someone else for the rest of our lives is, I believe, a better definition of marriage than the one we are likely to hear in more romantic descriptions.

I am not attempting to take feelings out of marriage. As a wise counselor once put it, "If it were not for the attractions and good feelings, two people would never want to undertake the hard work of building a

> **Attraction without commitment may be exciting but it won't bring much happiness.**

life together." I am not for a minute trying to play down the role of feelings. Feelings are just as much a part of us as our thoughts are. For too long "religions" and "churches" have too quickly labeled as "sinful" feelings that are simply a part of being human. As a happily-married couple said to me shortly before I was ordained, "If God created anything better than sex, He must have kept if for Himself." Feelings are good indicators for our lives. God speaks through our feelings too! But feelings cannot be the sole indicators of our lives. Attraction without commitment may be exciting but it won't bring much happiness. Feelings without thoughts are like a horse with no rider. There may be a lot of energy and movement but no direction or purpose.

Friendship is worth the effort of spending time getting to know someone else, of making ourselves vulnerable to that person in our feelings and thoughts, of being willing to forgive and be forgiven. We humans are never without some selfish motives, but friendship helps us to minimize our self-concern by showing concern for another self. People have lived their whole lives without getting married, but no one has lived very long or very well without friends. When friendship and love are combined in marriage then there really is something about marriages made in heaven!

As I struggled with this matter, my mind kept drifting back to a letter I wrote to my niece when she was in college. She was dealing with the typical adolescent and young-adult issues of peer pressure and premarital sex. I would like to close this chapter with that letter. I'm not sure I could improve on it.

Dear Suzanne:

I'm sorry I wasn't home when you wanted to talk. Your mother said you were really upset about a lot of the sexual activity on campus. The boys don't want to take you out unless you go to bed with them, and since there are other girls who do go to bed with them, that means you miss a lot of dates and parties. Your mother also mentioned that you didn't know how to keep answering all the questions a lot of your girlfriends were throwing at you — questioning why premarital sex was wrong.

Suzanne, I don't know anybody smarter than you, so I can't pretend to be able to give answers any more brilliant than you would give. Perhaps the real issue is not a matter of brilliant answers as much as it is a matter of people just not wanting to accept any answers. There are a lot of people who want to justify and rationalize their behavior, and they simply do not want to take seriously an opposing point of view.

Suzanne, we live in a nutty age. It's a time when all kinds of values have been turned upside down. There was a time, not long ago, when a girl who lost her virginity before marriage was really embarrassed by that. Today we live in an age when some people are far more embarrassed admitting their virginity!

If I were to offer answers as to why I think premarital sex is wrong, I would have to begin with my belief in God — a God I believe is so loving, so caring, so good, that He would only ask of us what was good for us. I don't picture God sitting in heaven and saying, "Hmmm, I wonder how I can make life miserable for humans. I know, I'll write some commandments." I think rather that God starts out loving us, and laws and commandments become the guidelines for experiencing love most completely in our lives, and for expressing our love for God most completely. And He didn't just give us laws. He promised to live within us to give us strength to keep His laws.

I know, though, that many of your friends and acquaintances don't believe in God, or, at least, they don't let that belief interfere with what they want to do. They might even laugh at you if you tell them that you do believe in God. I realize that for many today, sex is so casual that it seems no more a moral decision than blowing your nose. It's just something that involves good feelings and secreting some juices.

However, Suzanne, I hope you don't envy people who take sex casually. God didn't design us to be taken casually. We all come stamped

> **God didn't design us to be taken casually.**

"handle with care." When we stop handling each other with care, when we take people for granted and sex casually, then we lose the specialness of both sex and people. You see, sex is just a part of life. If we feel comfortable being selfish in our sexual attitudes and activities, then it doesn't take much to justify selfish activities in other areas of life. So we find people justifying cheating on tests, lying, stealing — in short, compromising other areas of their lives. Once we lose a standard of values in one area, we easily lower our values in other areas. In every civilization that has decayed from within, a lowering of sexual standards has been part of that decay. Self-discipline is part of self-love. Many of the people you see involved in a great deal of sexual activity really don't feel very good about themselves. I doubt if they would ever admit that to you.

You might be surprised to know, Suzanne, that there are people around you who envy you. You might get their envy in the form of putdowns, because anger is always a part of envy and jealousy. They envy the fact that you're willing to go without a few dates because you have self-respect. They envy the fact that you have a mind of your own, and are not caught up in all the social pressure of doing what everyone else does. They envy the fact that you're good-looking and full of fun, and still have an inner sense of personal strength. Quite frankly, they envy you because you do say "No." Many don't say no to premarital sex because they have no sense of self-respect, no real sense of values, no true belief in any God, and no real knowledge of the meaning and purpose of life. Your faith and your family have given you treasures many wish they had.

In all of my rambling, Suzanne, I'm really not sure if I've given you any new answers to your friends' questions. But I have one question you might ask them, and that is, "Are you really any happier because you've had sex?" I've never met anyone involved in consistent sexual activity outside of marriage who felt at peace. I've never met anyone involved in a promiscuous lifestyle who ultimately did not want to settle down. The tragedy of much of our society is that we are condi-

tioned to be perpetual children — preoccupied with ourselves, and our needs, and our pleasures. There are people who grow old but never grow up. It is possible to get addicted to selfishness in life, but always at a terrible price — the price of having lived life without ever knowing what life was all about.

In the back of my mind I recall an interview on a talk show with a professional call girl. The interviewer asked why she did what she did, and she replied that in addition to making a lot of money, she really enjoyed sex with varied partners. It was a lot of fun. This woman happened to have a baby daughter, and the interviewer asked, "Would you want your daughter to do this?" After a long pause the woman replied, "No." Sometimes life is not having all the answers. It's often a matter of having the right questions.

What you're struggling with, Suzanne, is trying to be a Christian in a secular world. And I can't imagine a time it has ever been harder. To some degree we're all influenced by it. I don't write this letter to you as one who has succeeded in being a perfect Christian. If I had waited until I was perfect, you would never have received a letter from me. All we can do in life is try. As Christians we're called not to let our successes make us self-righteous, nor to let our failures cause us discouragement. The incredible thing in life is not that we Christians sin too. The incredible thing is that we don't let our sins stop us from trying to be the best people we can be.

I'm convinced that God is not preoccupied with our failings. I am convinced that God is preoccupied with our love. In the scriptures,

55

when people were scandalized at Jesus associating with a sinful woman, he said, "Much is forgiven her, because she has loved much." A lot of the people around you are desperately searching for love in ways that only make them feel worse. They need love and understanding, not judgment. And they need your example, too, even if they would never admit it. They need to see someone who believes in God and feels loved by God, and who knows that love is always more than what flesh and blood can ever invent, or ever satisfy.

I wish it weren't such a struggle, Suzanne. I just wish being a Christian was a lot easier. But, then, God never said it would be easy. He just said that He would always stay with us.

Love,

Uncle Joe

CHAPTER SEVEN
Good and Evil

My seventh best guess about life is that God is on our side in the battle against evil! The "problem of evil" is probably the most discussed and debated issue among religious and non-religious people alike. If there is a God, how can He or She allow such bad things to happen? If God is good, how did the world get so bad? Books and treatises have been written and lectures have been given on the topic over the centuries! I can't pretend to say the last word in this single chapter. However, I hope I can say some helpful words that might make a difference when you think of God.

If God is good, how did the world get so bad?

One tendency in dealing with the problem of evil is to blame God for what goes wrong. In times of violent storms and earthquakes and mud slides and the like, insurance companies like to refer to "acts of God." If it's God's fault, don't expect us to pay for it, seems to be what they are saying! Blaming God is a handy answer, but is it the right answer? I think not.

If God caused bad things, what kind of God would He or She be? I recall watching a news clip about a bus full of children that had been involved in a terrible accident. Then I saw someone on the screen saying, "It was God's will." I remember feeling terrible anguish at those words. Who could believe in a God who injured or killed children? Who would want to spend any time with such a God on earth, much less spend eternity in heaven with such a deity? We put parents who abuse their children in jail. Is God a less loving parent than earthly parents? If we would not tolerate child abuse from other people, why would we tolerate such behavior from God?

A milder form of blaming God for evil in the world is saying that it is "God's way of testing us." The implication here is that we grow from our experiences of pain and suffering. While I firmly believe that we do mature through overcoming obstacles and tragedies, I cannot believe God causes them. What parent would test his or her child by injuring or starving or hurting the child? Why would we expect less of God than we would of ourselves? I believe that God is with us in the dark valleys of depression and tragedy, helping us to move through the valleys to the mountain peaks of light and love. I just don't believe God throws us in the dark valleys first to test us!

A third way of blaming God for what goes wrong is to say that it's all a mystery that we cannot comprehend now. In essence, this is the answer God gave in the book of Job, "Where were you when I created the world?" In other words,

While intimidation by authority is a time-honored tradition, I do not think God acts that way with us.

the author has God intimidate Job because Job is only a creature and God is God. What right does a creature have to question God? While intimidation by authority is a time-honored tradition, I do not think God acts that way with us. Other passages of scripture offer a different picture of God, such as God speaking through Isaiah, "Even if a mother should forget her child, I will never forget you." A wise scripture scholar once said, "There are so many contradictory passages in the scriptures as to keep any one of us from ever believing we have all of the truth." No doubt there will always be much to life and to God that will remain mysterious. While we cannot figure out the mystery of God, we should be able to count on the mystery. At the very least, God must be a mystery of love, a mystery on our side in life.

If bad things are not God's will, then where do they come from? Again, a comprehensive answer would literally take volumes, but for the purpose of this chapter let me list three answers. Tragedy and destruction are caused by:

1. The forces of evil;
2. Original sin;
3. Free will.

Let's examine these three separately.

"The forces of evil" is a generic term that sometimes gets personalized as the Devil, Beezlebub, or the Prince of Darkness, or is referred to more generally as cosmic forces or evil spirits. The point is that world religions consistently name a force opposed to God, a force of chaos that works against order, a force of destruction that works against creation. A work of art can be painstakingly crafted with enormous expenditure of time, energy, and resources, and then be destroyed in a single moment. Something like that works against

> I believe that good is stronger than evil, salvation is stronger than sin, life defeats death.

truth and beauty and goodness. Because I am a Christian, my belief system was formalized very early in life. Yet, as an adult, I see empirical evidence of something working against our best intentions. Just try to do something good and see how difficult it is!

Consequently, I do not believe in a morally neutral universe. I believe there are forces of good and evil, light and darkness, order and chaos, that contend with each other. With my Christian background, I believe that good is stronger than evil, salvation is stronger than sin, life defeats death. That is my ultimate belief. However, in day-to-day living, as I see and read of scenes of carnage and destruction, I never doubt the power of the forces of evil on any given day.

On the light side, when I think of our traditional understanding of the devil, I recall the story of the young wife who had just bought a new outfit. When her husband came home, he was furious. "Honey, you're busting our budget. You know we can't afford that." The wife responded, "But the devil made me do it." The husband replied, "Well, why didn't you just say, 'Get behind me Satan'?" The wife answered, "I did. And the devil said, 'That outfit looks great from the back too.'"

In discussing the influence of the powers of evil or the devil, I am not attempting to feed the tabloid frenzy concerning stories of demonic possession or devil worship. The devil has no power over our wills that we do not give to him. No one is ever possessed by the force of evil against his or her will. In fact, I would find it hard to imagine a single instance where the only explanation for someone else's behavior could be demonic possession. The bizarre behavior of individuals usually has other possible explanations. Borderline personalities and easily-influenced people may be attracted to demonic or devil-related activities, but usually there is a psychological explanation rather than a theological one. Too often, the devil is used as a handy way to avoid responsibility for our own behavior. The power of evil may influence us, but it cannot control us. While I do believe in the existence of the forces of evil, I do not believe that such a force or forces can ever take away our free will.

A second explanation for tragedy and destruction in the world is what Christians call original sin. I have already referred to original sin earlier as something that prevents us from always making the right decision. The scriptures describe in poetic fashion how something went wrong at the very beginning of human history and, as a result, the bond of trust was broken between God and man and man and woman. In a sense this disruption affected not only the harmony between God and humans and humans with each other, but it even reflected the disharmony between humans and animals and nature in general. Again, however we describe it, original sin simply reflects that something is wrong with the world. A wise person once commented that the only doctrine of the Church that is empirically verifiable is the doctrine of original sin. All we have to do is pick up a newspaper and we discover quickly that something is wrong with the world.

Finally, a third explanation for tragedy and destruction is free will. As a result of the influences of the forces of evil and of our own natures flawed by original sin, we make flawed choices. We can choose what is harmful to us and what is harmful to others. Most traffic accidents, for example, are the result of poor choices either to drive at excessive speeds, or to drive under the influence of some drug, or to operate without safe equipment. That God respects even our poor choices reflects God's permissive will, not His perfect will.

A point that some find helpful in this whole discussion is precisely the distinction between God's permissive will and God's perfect will. God's permissive will respects what He has created. So, for example, God respects the law of gravity, whether it is an apple or a plane falling to the ground. God respects our free choices, whether we make good ones or bad. God respects even the forces of evil in the sense that evil is the opposite of good. For God to choose to create people who were good, and a world that was good, was necessarily to set them in opposition to evil.

From a human point of view, God's decision to create was not too unlike each parent's choice today to have a child. We each know all that is wrong with the world, but we still choose life over death; we still choose to give someone the chance at life no matter how tough it may be. Creation seems to presume its opposite, even for God. For there to be up, there must also be down. To be North, there must also be South. To be light means there must be darkness. In a true act of love, a love not often meditated on or properly appreciated, God loved us enough to create us, because non-existence is worse than any pain. In other words, God had to know life would be tough for us, but he deemed a tough life better than no life. Love is not afraid of pain because love transforms pain.

The point of all of this is to put God on our side against the powers of darkness. From a Christian point of view, the best proof of God's love is that He did not remain aloof from His creation. Instead, He chose to become part of it in order to show us that He was not afraid of pain if it would show us how much He loved us. Even a God of love could not create a world free of hurt. This, I believe, is an insight uniquely possible from a Christian view of life. Many peoples and many religions throughout history have conceptualized the need to sacrifice a creature to a god or gods. However, only the Christian religion articulates an image of the one God who chose to sacrifice Himself for His creatures! This image of God puts God squarely on our side all during life. The word compassion comes from two Latin words meaning "to suffer with." God came to suffer with us to let us know that He was on our side to stay. And God will always be here to help us to resist evil, to endure evil, to overcome evil.

In terms of the visible world, the world that ends with physical death, evil at times seems stronger than death. This is why I consider the notion of eternal life critical. There is a world beyond this one where life is restored, where justice prevails, and where evil is forever vanquished. Here God's perfect will reigns; here is a world of kindness and justice and peace.

Belief in this world is not pie in the sky. (An image that always conjures up, in my mind, dessert being served on planes.) Rather, belief in another world gives fuller meaning to this world. An ideal world gives us direction and purpose in the real world. Here we are called to live in a way that helps that ideal world to break into our world. Here we live in the kingdom of earth trying to infuse it with the spirit of the kingdom of heaven. When we try to live like the God separate from us, we call forth the presence of God within us!

Now life begins to make sense. Instead of viewing the problem of evil as something to blame on God, we understand the problem of evil as something to be conquered by love, by the God within us. So when we ask, "Where is God?" or "Where was God?" the answer becomes clearer to us. God is within us, with us in the other people who love and care about us. In times of tragedy, God was in those people who stayed with us during our bereavement, who were in the ambulances and hospitals, who helped us rebuild our lives. When we can accept the notion of a loving God not afraid to get hurt loving us, then we can understand that the purpose of life is for each of us not to be afraid to get hurt in order to love and help each other!

The problem of evil, then, becomes less of a problem when we can move from viewing God as just "out there," at times seemingly unconcerned about our tragedies, to seeing God as present within us, moving us to be God by our gifts to each other of time, caring, feeding, nourishing, and housing. We have not been dumped on a planet to be tested by God and then die. Instead, we have been loved to life by a God who asks us to love each other all the way to death. Because of the realities of life we will do that imperfectly, which is why God's Spirit is always available to forgive and heal and renew us. The Spirit does this so we can forgive and heal and renew each other. Just as hell is the absence of God, so evil is the absence of good. But if we are filled with God, heaven conquers hell and good overwhelms evil.

Those who say that God is a mystery are absolutely right. But God is a friendly mystery, a mystery of life, love, and creative energy always on our side against the forces of death and destruction. God is really that good, and so are we! If only we would believe it. If only we would dare to live it!

CHAPTER EIGHT
Look for the Good

My eighth best guess about life is that there is good to be found in any situation. This is not meant to be a Pollyanna statement implying that all is well with the world. Following a chapter on the "problem of evil" it should be obvious that I take evil very seriously. Perhaps it is just another way of stating that God is to be found in every situation. There are two common enemies to this statement. The first is focusing only on what is wrong. The second is our tendency, at times, to miss the present moment, not to enjoy what we can of our lives right now. Let's look at these two separately.

Finding the good in any situation directly challenges the tendency to focus only on what is wrong. Perhaps too often on my weekly radio show I quote a favorite rhyming couplet, "Two men looked out through prison bars. One saw mud. The other, stars." In life, when times seem woeful, when we are in the prison of our own depression, or the prison of some calamity or tragedy, we still have choices. We can choose to look at the mud, at what is wrong, and make worse our sickness or despair. Or we can look at the stars. We can focus beyond ourselves at what can be. We can focus on our ideals, on a better future. We can imagine a time when things will be better.

In talking to teenagers it is so important to repeat the sentence, "Things will not always hurt this much." As adults we know the storm clouds will pass, the mud will dry, the prison doors will spring open. Life teaches us that things do not stay the same. Often our young people cannot know that. They imagine that the pain they feel at the present moment, no matter what the cause, will be with them the rest of their lives. We need to tell them that things will not always hurt this much. We need to believe that ourselves.

A cynic once challenged a believer to explain where she found God. The believer replied, "I see God the Creator in the beauty of a sunrise, in the grandeur of

> "Where do you find God when you look at the ghettos?"

a sunset, in the majesty of towering mountains, in the loveliness of a tropical island." The cynic replied, "Where do you find God when you look at the ghettos, at people living in substandard housing, at the homeless on the street, at the drug addicts and winos? Where do you find God there?" The believer responded, "There I see the suffering Christ, the God who suffers at the hands of our cruelty, our lack of caring, our lack of a sense of justice." God is there in each situation. It takes eyes of faith, however, to always see God.

On a personal level, I recall a woman suffering in the last stages of disease. She said, "I consider it a privilege to suffer, to be able to identify my sufferings with what Christ experienced on the cross. I offer up my sufferings to God for others so that others might be strengthened." Here was someone able to find good where someone else might be tempted to despair. As Victor Frankl, the Nazi concentration camp survivor, said, "If we have a why we will find a how." In other words, if we have a purpose to our lives, we will find a way to make sense of life, no matter how difficult.

There is good in every day, in every person, in every situation. There is good there because God is there. It is not just a matter of discovering God in a particular situation, but in realizing that we bring God to each situation. In a very real sense, each situation is better because we are there! This does not mean that we enter a situation of terminal illness or tragedy and offer pious platitudes or suggest positive thoughts. "Oh, don't worry. Things will get better" — such advice helps no one. To bring God to every situation may mean simply to bring our listening presence to some hurting person. The greatest comfort we bring to someone in pain is rarely the words we say, but the fact that we were there.

Another important technique that helps us to see the good in any situation is to keep some perspective. One of my favorite examples of perspective is a letter a daughter sent home from college to her parents:

Dear Mom and Dad:

The dormitory I'm living in burned down last night. The fire started in my room where my roommate and I were smoking pot together. My boyfriend said not to worry, that I could move in with him! I had intended to move in with him anyway after the baby was born. He has no job and has never worked, but I love him so. His father said we could live in a small apartment he has over his gas station. The gas station is in Anchorage, Alaska!

Love,
Your daughter, Cathy

P.S. None of the above is true. The dormitory did not burn down. I do not smoke pot. I am not pregnant. I am not moving in with my boyfriend. I am not moving to Anchorage, Alaska. However, I did flunk chemistry! I just wanted to put that in perspective.

Perspective may not always help us to see all the good in any situation, but it can help us not to see too much bad. It reminds me of the story of the funeral of the meanest person in town. At the funeral, the minister asked anyone who had anything good to say about Bill to please do so. There followed an uncomfortably long silence. Finally, an old fellow stood up and said, "Well, sometimes old Bill weren't as bad as he usually was."

When times are tough we may not always be able to see the good, but it is helpful to see less evil. A sign in front of a church once read, "Do we ever thank God for what did not happen to us?" One old parable speaks to the heart of the matter. A man was complaining bitterly to God about the heavy cross he had to bear in his life. God said to him, "There's a large room over there full of crosses. Go in through this door and leave your cross, and then go through that door to pick a new one." Happily the man dropped his cross in one door, and quickly entered by the other door to get a new cross. Much to his dismay, many of the crosses towered above him, and were so heavy he could not begin to carry them. Finally, he spotted one small cross that looked pretty easy to handle, so he asked God for that cross. God replied, "My son, that is the cross you brought into the room."

Seeing the good in any situation not only helps us to put our own problems in perspective, but it helps us realize that we bring good to situations. No matter

The good is in those who help others recover from disaster.

what calamity or flood or war or earthquake anywhere on the globe, there are always scenes afterwards of money and personnel and help pouring in to assist. The good is not the particular disaster. The good is in those who help others recover from the disaster.

A second thing about seeing the good in every situation is that it helps us to live more fully in the now, in the present moment. Too often the moment I most often miss is the "right now" moment. It is so easy to be looking at the next moment that I miss the present one. In a sense, what I have been conditioned to do is to enjoy now only by looking back on it and savoring some good from it. Yet I know the futility of that. Tomorrow I will be busy with many things, forgetting to enjoy the moment of tomorrow. Eventually tomorrow's run out. In reality we only have the now to live and to enjoy.

What I am trying to do right now is to enjoy writing this chapter. Part of me says that I will only be able to enjoy it when and if I see it in print some day. Yet what an awful thing to do to myself. Working to craft ideas, working as a "wordsmith," as one person described it, is worth doing even if no one ever sees my words. Like wild flowers that grow in the weeds and woods whether or not anyone notices or appreciates them, I have to appreciate the beauty of what I do now or am trying to do. It's hard for me to do that. I often look at enjoyment as if it were dessert. I am to enjoy something only if and when I have first finished all my work.

Failure to enjoy the now is also captured in a story that a psychologist told. This particular individual was flying in an airplane when the pilot announced that because of strong head winds, the plane would arrive about an hour late. The psychologist pushed his chair back and decided to enjoy the extra hour of flight. He looked out the window and marvelled at the clouds and sky and the beauty of flight — of a monstrously heavy object sailing through space! Suddenly his reverie was broken by an awareness that all around him people were grumbling and getting angry. He heard some people commenting, "This airline is always late." He heard someone else worrying aloud about his connecting flight.

In the exact same situation, people were reacting very differently. He was enjoying the beauty of the moment. Others were fretting and worrying about the future. Neither fret nor worry did anything to appreciably change the reality of the plane's flight, but it certainly did something to destroy the peace of mind of those who fretted and worried. The doctor referred to this as "ruining the moment," as "wasting the now." In my chapter on no sin being unforgivable, I noted how some people can steal joy from their lives by brooding over the past. Here was an instance of how others could miss the now by worrying about the future. The behavior is counter-productive, but how often we all do it!

Something I find helpful in my own life that calls me back to the present moment is a little meditation written by Helen Mallicoat. Her meditation goes like this: "I was regretting the past and fearing the future. Suddenly my Lord was speaking, 'My name is I Am.' He paused. I waited. He continued. 'When you live in the past, with its mistakes and regrets, it is hard. I am not there. My name is not I Was. When you live in the future, with its problems and fears, it is hard. I am not there. My name is not I Will Be. When you live in this moment, it is not hard. I am here. My name is I Am.'"

Sometimes early life experiences weave patterns of worry into us. Sometimes we are high-strung — prone to be more anxious by our genetic makeup.

Sometimes early life experiences weave patterns of worry into us.

While we may not be able to reverse old patterns or deny our genes, we can at least lessen some of the tension. If we can accept that God is as good as God says He is, then we really can give the past to God. With the same logic, we can believe that a good God will be there when we get to the future. As a Black Gospel spiritual goes, "God didn't bring us this far to leave us now." And with the same simple faith, we can believe that God is with us right now and we will be okay.

Is this a simplistic statement that if we have faith we will never get hurt? The answer is obviously no. Good people do get mugged, and do get injured in accidents, and surely die of diseases. Faith does not guarantee a painless existence. It simply guarantees a meaningful existence. Faith does not protect us from hurt. Faith simply protects us from despair.

One of the distinct beauties of the Christian religion is that the lowliest person can still believe that God understands what he or she is experiencing. Even an abject person sitting on death row awaiting execution can know that God also knows what that feels like.

Seeing the good in the present moment and seeing the good in every situation is an act of faith in God. The pain will not last. Tragedy will not have the last word. Death is not the end. Life is resurrection, constantly coming back from the little deaths such as disappointment and divorce and job loss and finding new opportunities and a new partner and a new job. Faith that conquers the little deaths is the same faith that gets us through and beyond our final death. There is always hope because there is always the presence of God.

One final thought about living in the now. Now is the time to do all the good we can do. We all know good people who have

Now is the time to do all the good we can do.

died. We have seen once strong and vibrant people who had poured out their energies helping others, in their final moment having energy only to take the next breath. Now is the time to do good. Now is the time to consciously bring the God within us to whatever situation we find ourselves in. There is a famous quote that I heard early in life, and I hope I will try to live it until the end of life. It goes like this: "I expect to pass through this world but once. Any good, therefore, that I can do, or any kindness that I can show to my fellow creatures, let me not defer nor neglect it. For I shall not pass this way again."

CHAPTER NINE
Loving Ourselves

My ninth best guess about life is that our greatest enemy is often the enemy within. We treat ourselves in ways that we would never treat anyone else. Perhaps we have been taught to love others but not to love ourselves. There's a famous scene in an old Pogo cartoon in which the alligator comes back in battle gear with the famous statement, "I have met the enemy, and he is us."

I spent a previous chapter talking about self-forgiveness and my ten commandments for self-love. The aim in all of this is to respect the creation of God that we are! We must believe that we are made in the image of God. God is my Father, my Mother, my Brother or Sister, however I conceptualize God. I must see myself and my worth in relation to God. Having said much of this before, I simply want to reflect in this chapter on why we experience such resistance to self-love.

First, I believe that despite all the books and talks and therapy many of us stay stuck in patterns of self-hatred and self-destructive-

I must see myself and my worth in relation to God.

ness. Some of this may be rooted in poor theology and poor religious formation. In the minor seminary, for example, we had a religious exercise called *Particular Examine*. This amounted to an examination of conscience in the middle of each day. The examination was, of course, written in such a way that the individual always lost! For example, let's say that the examination was on prayer. The first question might read, "Did I pray too little today? Am I lazy?" Then the second question might read, "Did I pray too much today? Am I proud?" However you looked at it, you lost. What this did was to breed into sensitive souls a constant dissatisfaction with themselves. It was never enough. God became an unpleasable father. Even in our best efforts, we always felt like prodigal children.

Another spiritual exercise designed for self-loathing came from mandatory readings of the *Imitation of Christ*. This was a "spiritual classic" by Thomas Kempis which seemed to have at its core the belief that we give glory to God by thinking less of ourselves! Here we were in our adolescence being encouraged to think of ourselves in the lowest forms possible. I'll never forget a meditation, not directly from the *Imitation* but given to us by a priest, in which he likened "God becoming a man to us becoming a cockroach." What a beautiful description of humanity — a cockroach. With enough warm, positive thoughts like that in the impressionable years of adolescence, it was possible to have an attitude of self-dissatisfaction set for life.

Second, and obviously related to the first point, I believe that early negative conditioning may be more powerful than later positive reinforcement. In other words, early indoctrination

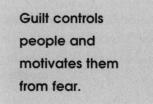

Guilt controls people and motivates them from fear.

with negative self-images predisposes us to respond more easily later in life to put-downs rather than to build-ups. I'm constantly amazed in preaching that it is always easier to make people feel guilty than it is to make people feel good about themselves. Part of why so many hell, fire, and damnation words and images were written into the Bible and incorporated by preachers into sermons is that guilt sells! Guilt controls people and motivates them from fear. Sometimes feeling guilty can feel more natural than feeling good or feeling free!

A third reason why we may have difficulty loving ourselves is that, as a result of a distorted notion of God and a distorted religious formation, we have a distorted notion of ourselves. Instead of hearing an outside, critical authority judge us or put us down, we internalize these voices. We put the enemy within ourselves! This masochistic voice, this self-destructive tendency, may be manifested in any number of ways.

First, our self-destructiveness may be manifest in our tendency to be perfectionists. This can be even a religiously-approved neurosis. "Be perfect as your Father is perfect" — we can quote the words of Jesus to put ourselves down. What a distorted notion of all He stood for! We forget that Jesus did not tell us to wait until our neighbor was perfect before we loved him or her. Why should we wait until we are perfect? Yet logic, kindness, and persuasion often do not succeed in getting us to love ourselves. Like a dog with a bone, we often won't let go of our self-destructive patterns.

A second way our self-destructiveness may be manifest is in our inability to forgive ourselves. Having done a chapter on this I feel no need to elaborate further. My favorite story on self-forgiveness, however, is about a priest who was giving spiritual direction to a woman. In the course of weekly counseling, the woman began to speak about visions she was having of God. To do a little reality testing, to see if the woman was really talking to God and not just hallucinating, the priest said to her, "The next time you talk to God, why don't you ask Him what my sins are?" A few days later the woman returned, and the priest asked her, "Well, did God tell you what my sins are?" The woman replied, "No. God told me to tell you that He's forgotten your sins." In our self-destructiveness we may be carrying around in our minds things which God has long ago forgiven and forgotten.

A third way our self-destructiveness may be manifest is when our lack of self-worth leads us to act in ways that seem to prove our worthlessness. Unfortunately, we will act the way we think. If we think we are no good, we will act that way. One of the saddest examples is the story of a girl who was among the brightest and best in high school. Yet, her

> **If we think we are no good, we will act that way.**

parents told me, she never seemed to like herself. In her senior year, she met an older man who introduced her to an entirely different way of life than she had known. He introduced her to alcohol and then to harder drugs. He got her to move out of her family home and to move in with him. With her mind messed up with drugs and booze he got her a job as a dancer in one of the nightclubs on Baltimore's Block, a sleazy section of town. It was a short step from there to becoming a prostitute on the block. One night in desperation the girl called her mother and cried, "Oh, mom, I wish I were away from all of this. I wish I were a little girl again." That night she took an overdose of drugs.

I can never forget that story. It stays stuck in my mind as a parable of the power of self-destructive thinking and behavior. How much we need to convict others of goodness, not of sin! How much we need to convince others of their specialness!

How easy to say those words, how desperately we need to hear them, but how difficult they are to live. I believe the cure lies in reworking our self-imaging and self-perception. We need to pay attention to our mental diet! What am I feeding myself each day of life?

As I worked on these ideas, I was walking around on a beautiful day, feeling fine, when suddenly a single thought went through my mind, and I was in depression. If a thought has the power to depress me, then a thought must also have the power to pick me up! We must listen to our mental diet. What do I say to myself when I do something wrong? Am I harsh and critical and cruel? No one else can control our thoughts. We must start to allow healing thoughts to replace hurtful thoughts, to allow positive thoughts to replace negative thoughts, to allow God-loving thoughts to replace self-hating thoughts.

A lady shared with me this technique to bolster self-esteem. She began each day with four positive thoughts about herself; as she went to bed, she closed each day by thinking of four different things she had done that day and feeling good about them. They may not have been spectacular things. They may have been holding a door for someone, letting someone into a line of traffic, baby-sitting for a friend, or whatever. The point is that she began to replace self-criticizing thoughts with self-esteeming thoughts. We have to do this consciously until these thoughts begin to replace the self-destructive thoughts we have unconsciously.

Again, there is no simple technique to healing ourselves of self-destructive attitudes and behaviors. We need good friends, occasionally good therapists, and always new learning experiences. As a wise person said, "If we keep doing what we always do, we keep getting what we always got." Self-healing involves new thoughts and new behaviors. Guilt and fear may be comfortable, but they are still a prison. Living in new ways and loving in new ways may seem risky, but they are the way to freedom and joy!

Ultimately, healing results from our relationships. There are dozens, even hundreds, of schools of therapy, and what seems to work in all of them is the relationship of trust between therapist and client. We are healed in our human relationships. We are healed in our relationship with God. We need to invite a good God to be a part of our lives, to do for us what we cannot do for ourselves. So I would like to close this chapter with two healing prayers which may help us to make friends with the enemy within. We need to internalize a self-affirming, self-esteeming friend. We must be in touch with the God within so that God can become our own best friend.

These two prayers are simply entitled "Healing Prayer" and "Healing Prayer at Bedtime." I have adopted and adapted them from the Healing Ministry established and directed in Baltimore by Father Larry Gesy.

Healing Prayer

Lord, I ask you to enter into my heart and release me from those life experiences that torment me. You know me so much better than I know myself. Bring your love to every corner of my heart. Wherever you discover the wounded child, touch, console, and release me.

Walk back through my life to the very moment when I was conceived. Bless me again as I was being formed within my mother's womb and remove all barriers to wholeness which may have affected me during those months. Bridge the gap between the love that I needed and never perceived receiving.

Lord, I ask you to surround my infancy with your light and heal those memories which keep me from being free. If I needed more of a Mother's love, send me your Mother, Mary, to provide whatever was lacking. If I needed more of a Father's love and security to assure me that I was wanted and loved very deeply, I ask you to hold me and let me feel your strong protective arms. Give me renewed confidence and courage to face the trials of the world because I know my Father's love will support me if I stumble and fall. Thank you, Lord.

Healing Prayer at Bedtime

Lord, through the power of the Holy Spirit I release to you my memory as I sleep. Every hurt that has been done to me, heal that hurt. Every hurt that I have ever caused to another person, heal that hurt. All the relationships that have been damaged in my whole life, and I have buried deep within me, heal those relationships.

I choose to forgive by the power of the Holy Spirit dwelling within me, and I ask to be forgiven. Remove whatever bitterness or behavior pattern that I have developed as a result of my attitude of unforgiveness. Forgive me, Lord, for the times I did not want to forgive.

Lord, fill the empty spaces with your love.

Thank you, Lord.

Ultimately, the enemy within is defeated only by surrendering — to the God within!

CHAPTER TEN

Loving Our Neighbors

My tenth best guess about life is that it is important to think the best of others. Thinking the best of others means looking for the best in others.

Obviously there's plenty of stuff that's wrong with all of us. The surprise is not that the press can dig up dirt on someone. The surprise is that we can all rise above the dirt! As some wise person once said, "There is so much good in the worst of us and so much bad in the best of us that it keeps any one of us from judging the rest of us!"

The world needs less judgment and much more love. If I could reduce the Jewish Christian philosophy to one sentence it would be, "As God has treated us, so we should treat each other."

Why do we find it so hard to love others, even hard to love those we are closest to? I think there may be a number of reasons.

First, it's easy to slip into seeing people as burdens rather than as special people needing our love. One of my favorite cartoons is from *The Family Circle*. It shows a hassled mother with three children all pulling her in different directions. One child is crying, another holding onto her mother's pant legs with sticky fingers. Around this scene of mayhem are a couple of dogs barking. Beneath the picture there reads this caption: "Lord, give me the patience to endure my blessings."

A second challenge to loving others is that the demands of others can wear us down. No matter how excited and committed I am to helping people develop their spiritual life, to helping people discover their own worth and dignity in relation to God, I can't pretend that I'm thrilled by every phone call or letter or request for my time. There are days when the ministry feels like being eaten alive by millions of piranha. I have to find rest and distance and space for myself, as Jesus did, if I'm to help others.

Sometimes even our highest ideals do not help us in this area. I recall a true story of a Retreat Master who responded to every phone call with the words, "It is the Lord." He had trained himself to see every demand on his time as coming directly from God — surely a noble effort. One of the ladies on Retreat loved this insight. She returned home following this prayerful weekend to be greeted by a ringing telephone. Telling herself, "It is the Lord," she answered the phone — only to get an obscene phone call! Our best intentions and our highest ideals do not always help.

Her story reminds me of another story about a brilliant scientist who succeeded in making a clone of himself, a perfect imitation. The clone was like the doctor in every way possible, except for one: it used foul and obscene language. Since people were mistaking the clone for the doctor, the scientist became more and more embarrassed and agitated. Finally he took the clone to the top floor of the laboratory and pushed it out of the window. The scientist was later arrested for making an obscene clone fall!

There is the story of a harried priest who viewed all the calls and demands on his time as distractions from his real work. It was not until he adjusted his viewpoint that he discovered that distractions were his work.

Sometimes we simply have to distance ourselves from demands so that we can renew our perspective. Prayer really helps in this regard. I think of a teacher who always used to approach examination papers with great relish. Here was a chance to get back at certain students who continually misbehaved or disrupted the class. What this teacher taught himself to do was to pray for the students before checking the papers, and then to look first for what was right! Sometimes we have to create proper perspective, as well as proper distance, to cope with constant demands.

A third challenge to seeing the best in others, to really loving other people, is when we see them as competitors. This may be one of the most lethal aspects of our competitive culture. We are so wired to compete that we forget how to care and cooperate. Competition can threaten our relationships with our peers, our families, even our friends. Competition can even threaten the lives of "religious" communities. People band together to help others, but don't always like each other. We like to help others but we don't always like the other helpers!

The roots of our competitiveness with others usually rest in our personal lack of self-worth. Most of us are sufficiently insecure at some level that some very early residues of sibling

The roots of our competitiveness with others usually rest in our personal lack of self-worth.

rivalry in childhood can get kicked up in our adulthood. We can envy someone else's success. We can be jealous of the attention someone else is getting.

We can react in any number of ways. We can get into our hurt child routine and sulk. We can get into our angry routine and tear others down. We bad-mouth them and point out all their flaws. As I quoted earlier, "You don't have to blow out someone else's candle to make your light shine brighter." Yet, that is precisely what we do or are tempted to do. Gossip falls under this heading too. Gossip basically is confessing someone else's sins! Confession of our own sins may be declining in popularity, but confession of the real or imagined sins of others is more popular than ever.

What is the antidote for feelings of envy and competitiveness? Basically, we recognize that failure to appreciate the goodness and gifts and talents of others lies in our lack of self-worth. I envy to the degree I do not love myself. I begrudge others their talents to the degree that I do not appreciate my own talents. I gossip about others in the hope that others will not look at my faults! (A vain hope, incidentally; as the Arab Proverb goes, "He who gossips to you will gossip about you.")

In the past chapters I have discussed a number of suggestions for building self-esteem. Besides building up our sense of self-worth, something else that really helps is developing our sense of compassion. We are in this together, and no one gets a free ride. I firmly believe that if we could just realize how short life is, and how tough life is for all of us, that we would be so much kinder to each other. If we could just live life from the perspective of our deathbeds, how few things would really bother us in life. I have been around many dying people and I have yet to hear a single person talk about their wealth or power or fame. What they speak of are family, friends, and loved ones. There's more than enough grief in life for all of us. We really don't need to add to it by bad-mouthing or putting each other down.

There's a powerful quote from Emerson which goes something like, "If you could look into the heart of your worst enemy and see all of the accumulated hurt and pain there, you would be reduced to tears." In twenty-six years of counselling and hearing confessions, I have found nothing to refute that statement. The package is rarely the person. The appearance is seldom the reality. People carry terrible pains and fears and worries within while smiling on the surface. The person you think has it all together may be just a good actor. Ironically, the person you envy may be envying you!

Compassion teaches us to give each other the benefit of the doubt. Yes, our gifts vary, but they are all important. Yes, someone else may have a position of fame or prominence or prestige. So what? A wonderful meditation to keep perspective on yourself as well as on others is to try to imagine who was on the very spot you are on 3,000 years ago. We might make some general guess, but actually we know nothing of any individual who once stood where we now stand. Then ask yourself what anyone will know of you 3,000 years from today. The answer is the same. No one will know a thing about you or me. True, a few figures live in history books and are immortalized in statues or in pictures. But at best they are curiosities! They are the rarest of exceptions. For every pharaoh we can name who built the pyramids, there are hundreds of unnamed laborers who actually worked on them. As the proverb goes, "Better a live beggar than a dead king." Ultimately, we are important only to God. We matter to God. God never forgets us.

Building up our personal sense of self-worth helps us to love others. Learning compassion for others as we reflect on how short life is, and how tough life is for all of us, also helps us to love others. One final insight that has worked for me is an insight I gleaned from a lecture given by a priest from India.

This particular priest said, "When you Westerners hear God's command to love your neighbor as your self, you tend to think it means that as I love my individual self is a measure of how I should love your individual self." The speaker then went on, "That is a Western concept based on your emphasis on the individual. An Oriental approach to that command, and Jesus as a Semite was more Oriental than Western in thought, would understand that passage entirely differently. What they would understand Jesus as saying was that we are all part of the same self. In other words, the self is what we share. To see my neighbor hungry, then, is to see my self as hungry, so of course I would feed my neighbor. To see my neighbor thirsty is to see my self as thirsty, so of course I would give drink."

My recollections of that talk have changed my whole understanding of life. To see that we are in this together as part of the same self changes my world view of God, of others, and of myself. Now I read passages such as "What you do to the least, you do to me" in a whole new way. Ultimately, there is no least among us! There is only God among us! For God would create only in His image. For God to redeem would be to restore the Divine image in all of us. For God to send us His spirit would be simply to confirm the spark of the divine already present in each of us.

What we do to each other is what we do to God. That obviously offers a new awareness of how we behave morally. However, looking at it another way, we realize that what others do to help us is the divine presence working in our lives! When others ask where God is, I can only point to the person listening to their cry, offering comfort, bringing help. In the Christian scriptures, in the Gospels, we see miracles worked by Jesus instantaneously. God still works some healing through us. A speech therapist might spend months helping a stroke victim to utter a few words, but "the dumb are speaking." A physical therapist might spend months helping an injured person to walk again, but "the lame are walking." An eye surgeon might be able to perform a delicate operation on the retina, but "the blind are seeing." We hear of breakthrough discoveries in hearing aids, sign language, and new treatments for the deaf, but "the deaf are hearing." God is working miracles through us and around us every day. He works through believers and non-believers alike. But God is working, if we only take the time to notice. Believing that God is in each of us, that we are literally part of the same self, and that self is a part of God, changes how we view what we do, and how we view what is done to us. People who hurt or who are cruel or who steal are people who do not believe God is in them and who do not act on

> **What we do to each other is what we do to God.**

that belief. We need prisons and other measures to protect society from such people, but we can never give up on them. While they may not even know or even care that God is in them, we must not forget that He is in them. Eventually, they must be convicted of their goodness, so that they can begin to return all the good God has given them.

EPILOGUE

It is my firm belief that life is a process of discovering God everywhere. The pain of society results so often from taking God out of everything. Good things become destructive. When we take "GOD" out of "GOOD" we are left with "0" (Zero, Nothing). Sex that should lead to love, fun that should lead to fellowship, drugs that should lead to health, all leave us with anxiety and depression and sadness because we have emptied good of the presence of God.

It's a challenge putting God back into life. Or, to put it more exactly, it is a challenge seeing God everywhere when we have grown so accustomed to not seeing Him anywhere. If you are a bit more at ease with the notion of God as a result of reading this book, then perhaps I have done my part. Life is a process of self-conversion. We keep searching for God until we discover He's been with us the whole time. When we finally allow God to break into our lives, then we fall in love forever!

CHURCH FINDER

FREE Church Locator Service:

To Find The Nearest Roman Catholic Church To You:

Dial Toll Free:

1-800-MASSTIM (1-800-627-7846)

INDEX